Animal World

CONTENTS

MONKEYS AND APES

LARGEST APE

Gorillas are the largest apes. They are majestic animals, usually found in the jungles of Africa. Adult male gorillas grow to a height of 5.6-6 ft (1.7-1.8 m) and weigh up to 400 lbs (181 kg)! They have a black or brownish-gray fur and male gorillas develop a silver patch as they mature. Due to their bulky size, gorillas cannot travel from tree to tree and prefer to stay on the ground. They move around by 'knuckle walking', using both their legs and long arms. These huge apes eat as much as 50 lbs (22 kg) of food each day! Their diet consists mainly of leaves. Often portrayed as ferocious, they are actually quite shy and social. They are quite intelligent and communicate with one another using many sounds and gestures.

Did you know?

The howler monkey, found in the Amazonian rainforest, is not only the loudest monkey but also the loudest land animal! You can hear its call up to 3 miles (4.8 km) away! Howler monkeys call out to communicate with other members of their group and also to warn them of danger.

SMALLEST APE

The gibbon is the smallest ape known to man. The male gibbon grows to a height of around 3 ft (90 cm) and weighs between 12-20 lbs (5.5-9 kg). Gibbons are very good at jumping from one tree to the other and are quite slender with long arms. They have a brown to brownish-black fur and are known as lesser apes because of their small size. The largest among them is a species known as siamangs, which weigh about 30 lbs (13.5 kg). These apes do not like uninvited guests in their territory and often fight with intruders. In the wild, gibbons live up to 35-40 years.

SMALLEST MONKEY

The smallest living monkey is the Pygmy marmoset. Its length, excluding the tail, is between 4.3-5.9 in (11-15 cm) and it weighs 4.2-6.7 oz (120-190 g). These little monkeys are very fast and have special claws to help them climb trees. Their favorite meal is tree sap.

LARGEST MONKEY

The colorful mandrill, the world's largest monkey, can grow to a height of 3.3 ft (1 m)! Male mandrills can weigh up to 60 lbs (30 kg). Female mandrills are usually half the size of their male counterparts. Mostly found in the jungles of Africa, mandrills have a red and blue nose, golden beard, red lips, and olive green fur with a bright blue rump. Their skin color brightens as they get more excited. These monkeys enjoy roaming on the ground and climb trees only to defend themselves or to sleep. Mandrills are omnivores, although plants forms the bulk of their diet.

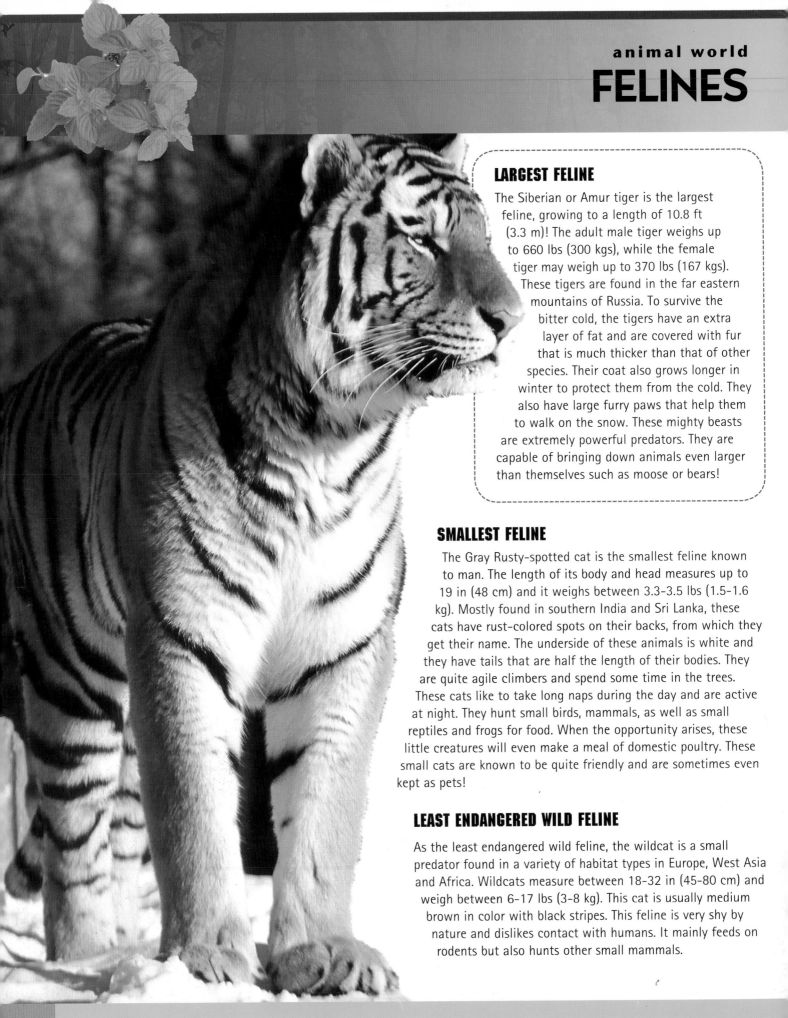

LARGEST FELINE

The Siberian or Amur tiger is the largest feline, growing to a length of 10.8 ft (3.3 m)! The adult male tiger weighs up to 660 lbs (300 kgs), while the female tiger may weigh up to 370 lbs (167 kgs). These tigers are found in the far eastern mountains of Russia. To survive the bitter cold, the tigers have an extra layer of fat and are covered with fur that is much thicker than that of other species. Their coat also grows longer in winter to protect them from the cold. They also have large furry paws that help them to walk on the snow. These mighty beasts are extremely powerful predators. They are capable of bringing down animals even larger than themselves such as moose or bears!

SMALLEST FELINE

The Gray Rusty-spotted cat is the smallest feline known to man. The length of its body and head measures up to 19 in (48 cm) and it weighs between 3.3-3.5 lbs (1.5-1.6 kg). Mostly found in southern India and Sri Lanka, these cats have rust-colored spots on their backs, from which they get their name. The underside of these animals is white and they have tails that are half the length of their bodies. They are quite agile climbers and spend some time in the trees. These cats like to take long naps during the day and are active at night. They hunt small birds, mammals, as well as small reptiles and frogs for food. When the opportunity arises, these little creatures will even make a meal of domestic poultry. These small cats are known to be quite friendly and are sometimes even kept as pets!

LEAST ENDANGERED WILD FELINE

As the least endangered wild feline, the wildcat is a small predator found in a variety of habitat types in Europe, West Asia and Africa. Wildcats measure between 18-32 in (45-80 cm) and weigh between 6-17 lbs (3-8 kg). This cat is usually medium brown in color with black stripes. This feline is very shy by nature and dislikes contact with humans. It mainly feeds on rodents but also hunts other small mammals.

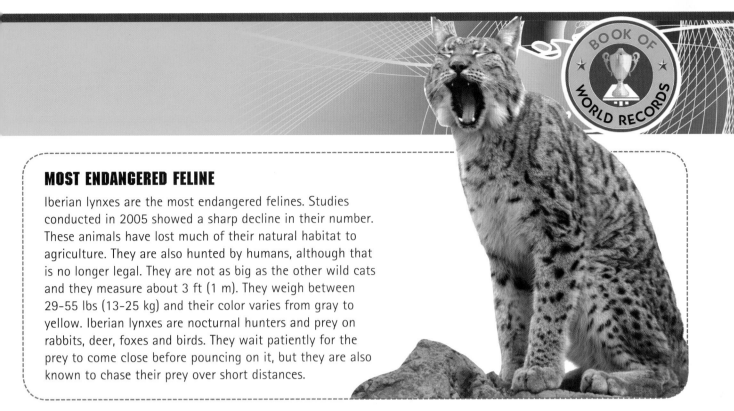

MOST ENDANGERED FELINE

Iberian lynxes are the most endangered felines. Studies conducted in 2005 showed a sharp decline in their number. These animals have lost much of their natural habitat to agriculture. They are also hunted by humans, although that is no longer legal. They are not as big as the other wild cats and they measure about 3 ft (1 m). They weigh between 29-55 lbs (13-25 kg) and their color varies from gray to yellow. Iberian lynxes are nocturnal hunters and prey on rabbits, deer, foxes and birds. They wait patiently for the prey to come close before pouncing on it, but they are also known to chase their prey over short distances.

Did you know?

The mountain lion holds the record for being the highest jumper. It is known to jump distances up to 18 ft (5.4 m) high! Its oversized paws and long tail helps it balance.

FASTEST FELINE

The fastest feline known to man is the spotted cheetah. It can cover 3.4 miles (5.5 km) at an average speed of 45 mph (72 km/h). The highest speed that a cheetah can reach is 71 mph (114 km/h). Every part of this magnificent animal is adapted for speed. Its claws are partly retractable to help it run fast. It also has a large heart designed to pump the blood quickly as it runs. Its tail is specially designed to help it change directions when its runs. It is usually yellow to light brown in color with round black spots and also has black marks around its eyes. The cheetah is mostly found in the African savanna, where the tall grass helps it to hide while hunting. The cheetah lives for about 14 years in the wild. They measure between 4-5 ft (120-150 cm) and they weigh about 90 lbs (43 kg).

HEAVIEST DOG

The heaviest dog in the world is the English mastiff. It weighs up to 200 lbs (90 kg) and can be as tall as 32 in (80 cm). These dogs have extremely powerful bodies with a square-shaped head. Their coat color is usually shades of fawn with black around the eyes, ears and nose. These muscular dogs are strong, courageous and usually very loyal to their masters. They are considered very good guard dogs. They are sometimes called gentle giants owing to their huge size but gentle nature.

FASTEST DOG

The fastest among all breeds of dogs is the greyhound. The fastest greyhounds can reach a speed of 45 mph (72.4 km/h) in 1.5 seconds. Greyhounds measure between 28-30 in (71-76 cm) in height and weigh between 70-100 lbs (27-40 kg). They come in a large variety of colors, the most common being shades of red, gray, black and white. They have a mild temperament and make excellent pets.

Did you know?

The most succesful mountain rescue dog was called Barry (1800-1814). It was a St. Bernard that worked as a mountain rescue dog at the monastery at the Great St. Bernard Pass. Barry saved the lives of over 40 people. The body is preserved at the Natural History Museum in Berne, Switzerland.

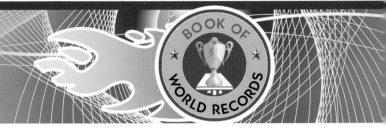

SMALLEST FOX

The smallest species of fox is the Fennec fox. Found in the hot North African desert, they have a unique way of keeping themselves cool — they extend the size of their ears! By doing so, the blood in their body reaches the surface of their large ears, where it is cooled. Their large ears also give them a good sense of hearing that helps them hunt well at night. The length of the Fennec fox varies between 14-17 in (36-44 cm). They weigh between 2-3.5 lbs (1-1.5 kg).

SMALLEST BREED OF DOG

Chihuahuas, the world's smallest dogs, get their name from a place in Mexico called Chihuahua where they were first found. On average, these tiny dogs grow to just 6-10 in (15-25 cm) tall, although some may grow up to a height of 15 in (38 cm). They normally weigh between 6-10 lbs (2.7-4.5 kg). They have eyes that are rather big for their tiny face. They also have striking ears that stand up straight. They may be short or long haired and come in a range of colors. Their small size makes them ideal pets.

LARGEST WOLF

The largest wolves in the world are Gray wolves. These large canines are between 4.5-6.5 ft (1.3-2 m) long from nose to tail, with a height of 26-36 in (60-90 cm). They weigh between 70-135 lbs (32-62 kg). They are found at high altitudes. These powerful wolves have great stamina and are known to travel long distances. They are usually white or gray, although some may be red, brown or black. They have excellent hearing and super sense of smell to help them hunt well.

HOOVED ANIMALS

BIGGEST ODD-TOED HOOVED ANIMAL

The biggest odd-toed hooved animal is the White rhinoceros. It is also known as the Square-lipped rhino because of its wide mouth, which it uses to nibble at plants. It can weigh up to 6,000 lbs (2,721 kg) or more! Its length, excluding the tail, is between 11-13.5 ft (3.35-4.2 m). These huge animals are found mostly in the grasslands and savannas of Africa.

BIGGEST EVEN-TOED HOOVED ANIMAL

The biggest even-toed hooved animal is the hippopotamus, often called the hippo. These bulky animals weigh between 3,300-4,000 lbs (1,500-1,800 kg)! These huge animals are typically 11 ft (3.5 m) long. Hippos are water-lovers and are usually seen submerged in water during the day. They come out of water only to graze. Despite their huge size, hippos are remarkably fast. They are known to run as fast as 25 mph (40 km/h)!

LARGEST ANTLERS

The moose is the largest member of the deer family and is the largest mammal in North America. The male moose has very large antlers. The largest that have been recorded were more than 6.5 ft (2 m) long! The moose has a lanky appearance owing to its long legs. The moose is a plant eater and enjoys grazing on young shoots and leaves of willow and birch trees.

FASTEST HOOVED ANIMAL

The fastest hooved animals are known as Pronghorn antelopes. They can reach speeds of 61 mph (98 km/h) and are second only to the cheetah in speed. They use their speed in order to protect themselves from predators. A fully-grown Pronghorn weighs between 75-145 lbs (35-60 kg). They are usually brown in color with white bellies. They have two white marks on their necks. Both male and female Pronghorns have horns. Pronghorns are fond of grasslands but can also be found in brushland and desert.

Did you know?

Caribous hold the record for being the land animals that migrate the longest distance in search of food. Their migration route takes them over 800 miles (1,300 km) each year! Wildebeest and zebra are second in line. In fact, wildebeest and zebras migrate together, sometimes forming groups of over a million members. This way they are able to protect one another from predators such as leopards.

Did you know?

Giraffes have the same number of bones in their neck as humans. The difference is each of the giraffe's seven neck vertebrae can be over 10 inches (25.4 cm) long!

TALLEST HOOVED ANIMAL

The tallest hooved animal is the giraffe. They are usually yellow in color with brown spots on them. They have very long necks which helps them to graze on tall trees. These animals are typically 16-19 ft (4.8-5.8 m) tall and weigh about 3,000 lbs (1,360 kg). They have double horns, usually 5 in (12.7 cm) long (although the female's are shorter), on their head which protects them in fights. Their diet usually consists of the leaves of the acacia tree. These tall ungulates are even-toed and mostly found in the savannas of Africa.

BIG AND SMALL ANIMALS

LARGEST BEAR

Found only on the Kodiak Archipelago near Alaska, USA, the Kodiak bear is not only the largest bear on earth but also one of the largest carnivores. When standing on four legs, these bears reach up to a height of 5 ft (1.5 m) and on two legs they reach up to 10 ft (3 m)! They weigh up to 1,500 lbs (680 kg). Kodiak bears mostly eat fish, but are also known to eat leaves, plants and berries. Although only very rarely, they have been known to attack humans.

LARGEST LAND MAMMAL

The largest land mammal is the African elephant. These huge animals stand 19.7-24 ft (6-7.3 m) high and weigh between 15,000-22,000 lbs (7,000-9,979 kg)! They are gray-brown in color, have a pair of huge tusks, a long trunk and large, fan-shaped ears. The size of their ears helps them to stay cool. Their trunks are made up purely of muscles and are used as a fifth limb for a number of tasks. Elephants use their trunks to break off branches for food, carry loads and even to spray water!

COLDEST BEAR

The polar bear is the only bear to survive in the freezing Arctic regions of the world. These bears can grow to 10 ft (3 m) long and weigh around 1,700 lbs (770 kg). Polars bears are well adapted to survive in the cold regions. They wear a thick coat of fur that keeps them warm. They also have a thick layer of blubber and fat that acts as extra insulation. Polar bears are white in color, which allows them good camouflage against their snowy surroundings. This is especially useful when they hunt, enabling them to catch prey such as seals. Polar bears are very good swimmers too and are even known to catch fish while underwater!

SMALLEST BEAR

Measuring between 47-59 in (120-150 cm) in length, the sun bear is the world's smallest bear. It is also known as the Malay bear and is usually black or brown in color. It weighs only about 88 lbs (40 kg). Although it is the smallest member of the bear family, the sun bear is known to be quite aggressive. It has very sharp canine teeth that are designed for tearing meat. The sun bear gets its name from the orange-yellow horseshoe-shaped burst of color around its neck.

LONGEST GESTATION PERIOD

Elephants have the longest gestation period in the world. They typically carry their young for up to 22 months before giving birth to a single calf. Newborn elephants usually weigh around 200-250 lbs (90-115 kg). They are able to stand on their own within an hour and can follow their mother after just a few days. Female elephants live in large groups. The members of a group share the responsibility of bringing up the baby elephants in the group. The calves suckle about 3 gallons (11 liters) of milk every day and gain weight quickly.

Did you know?

Polar bears are the world's largest predators. In the Arctic they top the food chain, spending most of their time hunting down their favorite food: seals. A single polar bear can consume 100 lbs (45 kg) of meat at one feed!

LARGEST CARNIVOROUS MARSUPIAL

The largest known meat-eating marsupial is the Tasmanian Devil. This animal often lets out terrible shrieks from which it get its name. The length of its body and head is between 20-30 in (51-78 cm). Its tail is about 10 in (25 cm) long. This carnivore weighs between 13-22 lbs (6-10 kg). They have very powerful jaws and large teeth to tear into flesh. Their fur is usually black in color with white patches on their back, shoulders and neck. Tasmanian Devils are indigenous to the eucalyptus forests of Tasmania.

ENDANGERED MARSUPIALS

Wombats are among the most endangered marsupials. In fact, there are only 100 known Hairy-nosed Wombats, all living in the protected Epping Forest National Park in eastern Australia. For much of the 20th century wombats were considered pests and the Australian government paid people to kill them. Fortunately, this practice has stopped but the grassland habitat the wombat needs to survive continues to be reduced by grazing sheep and cattle.

GLIDING MARSUPIAL

One of the few marsupials known to glide is the Sugar Glider. Sugar Gliders have a very thin layer of skin between their first toe and fifth finger. This acts like a wing which enables them to glide for great distances - sometimes over 165 ft (50 m)! They use their tails to change direction as well as for balance. Sugar Gliders are around 8 in (20 cm) long, weighing just 4-5.7 oz (120-160 g). They have dark stripes on the back of their blue-gray coats and are tree dwelling animals.

Did you know?

The smallest known marsupial in the world is the Long-tailed planigale. Also known as a Ingram's planigale, it rises to a height of just 2 in (5 cm) and weighs just 0.15 oz (4.3 g). It has an unusual head shape, which is very broad and deep. This helps the tiny creature hunt for insects in cracks in the soil.

LARGEST MARSUPIAL

The world's largest known marsupial is the kangaroo. They measure about 6 ft (1.8 m) high and can weigh up to 187 lbs (85 kg). They have very big feet, strong legs, short forelimbs and long tails to help them balance when they jump. They can jump as high as 30 ft (9.14 m) and their tail can be as long as 3 ft (1 m). Male kangaroos are usually red-brown in color, which lightens towards the tail. The female often has a blue-gray tinge. These animals are mainly nocturnal. Indigenous to Australia, kangaroos are recognized as the country's most commonly used symbol.

FASTEST MARSUPIAL

A female Eastern Gray kangaroo holds the record for the highest speed reached by a marsupial and they are known to reach speeds of up to 40 mph (64 km/hour). The Eastern Gray kangaroo is mostly seen in southern and eastern Australia. Its coat is usually gray in color. It is most active at dawn. This marsupial is also a good jumper. It can leap up to 30 ft (9.14 m) in one jump!

SMALLEST RODENT

Pygmy jerboas have tiny bodies and comparatively long tails. They are the smallest rodents in the world. They can be as small as 2 in (5 cm) in size. They have tails that are at least twice the length of their bodies. Their long tails help them jump amazing distances - up to 10 ft (3 m) in some instances. They are usually most active at night. There are about 25 species of Pygmy jerboas and they are mostly found in the dry regions of Africa and Asia.

RODENT WITH THE LONGEST LIFESPAN

The Eastern Gray squirrel is known to have the longest lifespan among all rodents. The age to which this squirrel can live has been recorded at 23 years. Eastern Grays vary between 15-20.7 in (38-52 cm) in length. They are gray in color, but some white and black examples have also been found. The Eastern Gray squirrel has a long bushy tail which measures about 6-9.8 in (15-25 cm). These squirrels have the ability to adapt to varied conditions. That is why they have thrived when introduced to different parts of the world. Originally they were found in eastern and mid-western United States.

RODENT WITH THE SHORTEST LIFESPAN

The vole, a small mouse-like rodent, has the shortest lifespan among all rodents. Voles do not usually live for more than 3-6 months, although some are known to live up to a year. The longest known lifespan of a vole is 18 months. Voles vary in length between 3-7 in (7.62-17.7 cm). They are active both during the day and at night. Their diet mainly consist of grass, roots, tubers, snails and other insects. They are found in parts of Asia, North Africa, North America and Europe. In America they are also called field mice or meadow mice.

RODENT WITH SHORTEST GESTATION PERIOD

The rodent with the shortest gestation period is the hamster. Their gestation period is only 16 days. Their babies have not developed eyes, ears or teeth when born. Even the hands and feet of the pups are not fully formed at birth. Hamsters are usually 2-11 in (5-27 cm) long and weigh about 32 oz (900 g). Their color varies from white to brown. They may have short or long tails. They are active mostly at night. They have a lifespan of 2-3 years. Owing to their small size, friendly nature and mild temperament, many species of hamsters are kept as pets.

LARGEST RODENT

Measuring about 40-52 in (102-132 cm) in length, the capybara is the largest rodent in the world. These huge rodents have barrel shaped bodies and weigh between 60-100 lbs (27-50 kg). Capybaras are very good swimmers and divers and have webbed feet for this purpose. They like to spend their time resting in mud. They have brown fur that dries very quickly. They have two long front teeth which keep growing for as long as they live. They often whistle or let out barks when they want to call one another.

Did you know?

The guinea pig has the longest gestation period among rodents. Their gestation period lasts for about 68 days, which is almost as long as that of a dog! The newborn are born with teeth and open eyes. They also have hair on their bodies. Many species of guinea pigs are quite popular pets.

WHALES AND DOLPHINS

LARGEST DOLPHIN

The largest member of the dolphin family is the orca. Orcas are also known as killer whales, but this is quite misleading because they aren't whales at all! They have streamlined bodies that taper at both ends, making them agile swimmers. They are fierce predators and use their speed and strength to kill their prey. They also have strong and sharp teeth. They can swim as fast as 30 mph (48 km/h) while hunting. Their length varies between 27-33 ft (8-10 m). They are very bulky and weigh between 8,000-12,000 lbs (3,600-5,400 kg). These animals are usually black in color with distinctive patches of white.

Did you know?

The Dal's porpoise is the fastest porpoise. They can reach speeds of up to 34 mph (55 km/h). These porpoises usually swim in pods of 10-20 individuals.

DEEPEST DIVING WHALE

The sperm whale is the deepest diving whale in the world. These huge whales are known to dive as deep as 3,200 ft (1,000 m) below the surface. They are fascinating creatures and also have the largest teeth and the biggest brain among whales. They may weigh between 44-55 tons (40-50 tonnes) and can grow to a length of 36-59 ft (11-18 m). The sperm whale is found in almost all the oceans of the world.

LARGEST WHALE

The blue whale is an amazing creature that is not only the largest whale, but also the largest and loudest mammal in the world! Their calls reach very high levels which allows them to communicate with one another over hundreds of miles. These huge whales grow to a whopping 110 ft (33 m) and weigh up to 200 tons (although this is rare and is contested by some marine biologists). A blue whale's tongue alone may weigh more than two tons! These magnificent mammals are blue-gray in color and feed mainly on krill and plankton. These majestic animals are endangered, with only about 10,000 left today.

SMALLEST DOLPHIN

Named after Sir James Hector, who examined the first specimen of this species, the Hector's dolphin is the smallest and rarest dolphin in the world. It is also known as the Maui dolphin. The female of this species is usually larger than the male. The Hector's dolphin may grow up to 5.6 ft (1.7 m) in length and weigh between 88.2-132.2 lbs (40-60 kg). They are mostly gray in color with a sprinkling of other colors.

SMALLEST WHALE

Measuring only 8.86 ft (2.7 m) long, the Dwarf sperm whale is the smallest whale in the world. These whales weigh 551 lbs (250 kg). They are in fact smaller than some large dolphins. Dwarf sperm whales are blue-gray in color with a lighter belly. They have very sharp and long teeth. They eject a red substance as a way of distracting predators. These whales are found mostly in warmer waters. They have a habit of staying very still in the water.

FARTHEST MIGRATING WHALE

Gray whales are known to migrate the farthest distances among all whales. After cold winter months spent off the coast of California these creatures move to the Bering sea for feeding during summer. These creatures travel as much as 7,452-12,420 miles (12,000-20,000 km)! They can grow to a length of 39-46 ft (12-14 m). They eat huge quantities of food in a day and weigh around 16.5-38.5 tons (15-35 tonnes). They are commonly found along the North Pacific coastline.

OTHER MARINE MAMMALS

LARGEST MANATEE

Manatees are large sea mammals that are closely related to elephants. They are also known as sea cows. The largest manatee ever found had length of about 13 ft (4 m) and weighed about 3,400 lbs (1,542 kg). Manatees have barrel shaped bodies that taper to paddle-shaped tails. They also have a pair of forelimbs called flippers to help them swim better. These creatures love feeding on seaweed and consume large quantities of it each day. In this way they help to keep waterways clear.

FASTEST SWIMMING PINNIPED

The California sea lion is a very fast pinniped that can reach speeds of 25 mph (40 km/h). They are also very good divers and can swim to depths of 322 ft (98 m). They are around 6.5-8 ft (2-2.4 m) in length and weight up to 858 lbs (390 kg). These sea mammals are quite intelligent and are often trained by humans when kept in captivity. Californian sea lions are hardy and adaptible animals and their numbers are growing steadily.

ONLY PINNIPED WITH TUSKS

Walrusses are not related to elephants but they have two huge tusks. The tusks can grow as long as 3.2 ft (1 m). The tusks have rings on them that roughly correspond to one year's growth. So you can tell the age of a walrus by counting the rings! Walrusses have thick skin that helps them survive in the cold. They also have mustache-like bristles around their mouth that help them sense the movement of prey when in water. These fast swimmers are about 8.5-13.1 ft (2.6-4 m) in length and weigh between 2,255-3,527 lbs (1,250-1,600 kg).

Did you know?

The most abundant seals are Crabeater seals. There are at least 12 million Crabeater seals in the world today. Contrary to their name, Crabeater seals do not feed on crabs! In fact, their diet consists almost entirely of krill. Crabeater seals spend their lives on the icepacks of the Antarctica.

SMALLEST ARCTIC SEAL

Ringed seals are very small sea mammals that are found in the cold Arctic regions. They are the smallest of all the Arctic seals. Their length varies between 3-5 ft (1-1.6 m). They can weigh anywhere between 70-200 lbs (32-90 kg). They have light gray coats with black spots. The spots are often surrounded by lighter rings – hence their name! They have small heads and plump bodies. They feed on a variety of fish found in the Arctic waters.

LARGEST SEAL

Southern Elephant seals are the largest pinnipeds in the world. Males can grow to 19.6 ft (6 m) in length and weigh up to 8,818 lbs (4,000 kg). Adult male Southern Elephant seals have a huge nose that resembles the trunk of an elephant, hence their name. They are also a similar color to elephants. The males use their nose to make loud, roaring noises. Elephant seals are excellent swimmers and spend most of their time in water.

SHARKS AND RAYS

BIGGEST RAY

Manta rays are the biggest rays in the world. They can grow to widths of 22 ft (6.7 m) and weigh up to 3,000 lbs (1,350 kg)! These rays do not have stings at the tip of their spine and are generally harmless to humans. A striking feature of the Manta ray is its huge mouth. The biggest Manta rays would be able to fit four men side-by-side inside! They have white underbellies and are blue or black on top. These rays are quite agile and are even known to broach the surface of the water at times. They are found mostly in tropical waters, particularly in coral reefs.

SMALLEST RAY

The Short-nose Electric ray is the smallest ray known in the world. They are only 4 in (10 cm) wide and are also very light, weighing only 1 lbs (0.5 kg). They are a similar size to a pancake! Electric rays can produce an electric current to shock their enemies.

FASTEST SHARK

Able to travel at speeds up to 60 mph (97 km/h), the Maco shark is the fastest shark in the world. It is dark blue in color, with a white belly. It is usually 5-8 ft (1.5-2.5 m) long, but some are known to grow as long as 12 ft (3.7 m)! The Maco shark weighs about 1,000 lbs (450 kg). It can move from the surface of the water to deep underwater with ease and is found mostly in tropical and temperate seas. Maco sharks are among the few species of sharks that are known to attack people.

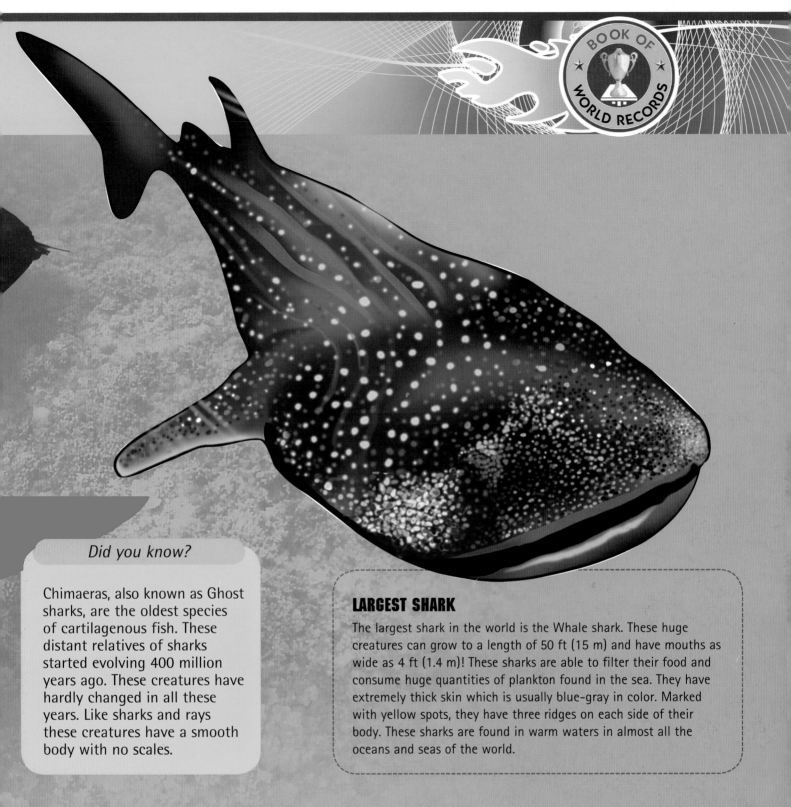

Did you know?

Chimaeras, also known as Ghost sharks, are the oldest species of cartilagenous fish. These distant relatives of sharks started evolving 400 million years ago. These creatures have hardly changed in all these years. Like sharks and rays these creatures have a smooth body with no scales.

LARGEST SHARK

The largest shark in the world is the Whale shark. These huge creatures can grow to a length of 50 ft (15 m) and have mouths as wide as 4 ft (1.4 m)! These sharks are able to filter their food and consume huge quantities of plankton found in the sea. They have extremely thick skin which is usually blue-gray in color. Marked with yellow spots, they have three ridges on each side of their body. These sharks are found in warm waters in almost all the oceans and seas of the world.

SMALLEST SHARK

The smallest (and probably the slowest) sharks in the world are the Pygmy Ribbontail catsharks. Their length varies between 6-7.5 in (15-19 cm). They are found at a depth of 229-2,460 ft (70-750 m). Pygmy Ribbontail catsharks are usually dark brown in color and have black patches on their dorsal fins. They are found in the Indian and Pacific oceans and feed on fish, crustacea and squid.

LONGEST STURGEON

Russian sturgeons are the longest sturgeons in the world. These fish can grow up to a length of 6ft (1.8 m) and weigh around 250 lbs (113 kg). Their bodies look like long spindles and they have short and rounded snouts with a lower lip. They are usually found in the Caspian Sea and the Black Sea. Due to overfishing their numbers are dwindling. Russian sturgeons produce the finest caviar that can sell for up to $200 an ounce.

ONLY MALE ANIMAL TO REPRODUCE

Seahorses are the only animals in the world where the male gives birth to babies! For this the male seahorse is equipped with a pouch called a brood sack, in which the female lays the eggs. The eggs hatch into babies in the pouch. Male seahorses show off their pouches to the females during the mating season to attract them.

Did you know?

Surpassing even the cheetah, the fastest land animal, the Cosmopolitan sailfish is the fastest fish in the world. They are capable of speeds of up to 68 mph (109.4 km/h)!

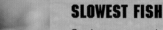

SLOWEST FISH

Seahorses are the slowest fish in the world. They move at speeds of just 0.009 mph (0.016 km/h). They are quite small in size, typically just 1.9-13.7 in (5-35 cm) in length. Their eyes are on the sides of their head, helping them to spot prey. Seahorses can also hunt without moving. They have long snouts with which they suck in their prey. Due to their small size they are easily swept away by water currents. In order to prevent this they have long tails which they can curl around seaweed. Some species are kept as pets but they do not survive very long.

SMALLEST CRAB

The smallest crab in the world is the Pea crab. They grow only to 0.25 in (0.6 cm). These crabs, sometimes called Oyster crabs, are found inside oyster and mussel shells. They have flaps around their tails which they use to protect their eggs. They are usually found in Scandanavia, Africa and the Mediterranean.

HEAVIEST BONY FISH

The heaviest bony fish is the Ocean sunfish. These weigh as much as 4,400 lbs (1,995 kg) and may extend to a length of 10 ft (3 m). They have a flat body which looks oval when seen from the front. This makes them look a little like the sun – hence the name. These curious looking fish have two large fins, enabling them to glide through the water. Their favorite food is jellyfish, which they consume in large quantities. Ocean sunfish come in a wide range of colors, ranging from brown to a silvery gray. They are found in all the temperate and tropical oceans and seas in the world.

BIRDS OF PREY

FASTEST FLYING BIRD

Peregrine falcons are the fastest birds in the world, capable of speeds of 124 mph (196 km/h)! Some have even been recorded flying as fast as 168 mph (270 km/h) when chasing prey. Peregrine falcons range in length from 13-20 in (34-50 cm) and they weigh between 18-32 oz (500-900 g). Peregrine falcons have long pointed wings and can fly at high altitudes. They often dive on their prey at high speeds. They feed on a variety of birds, such as pigeons, ducks, sparrows and starlings.

THE LARGEST NEST

The largest tree nest built by a hunting bird is that of the Bald eagle. Their nests can weigh as much as 3 tons (2.72 tonnes)! The largest examples measure 20 ft (6 m) in depth and 9.5 ft (2.9 m) in width. These hunting birds are the national symbol of the United States of America. Their heads and tails are white and their bodies are brown. They have huge talons on their feet and bright yellow eyes. They use their talons to snatch up fish from the water. These powerful and mighty birds are found in most of North America and have a stable population due to conservation efforts.

HEAVIEST BIRD OF PREY

Found in the Andes mountains, Andean condors are the heaviest birds of prey. They weigh between 16-33 lbs (7.5-15 kg) and their length ranges from 46-53 in (117-135 cm). They are usually completely black in color, except for a white patch around their neck. Their talons are not as sharp as most birds of prey and they tend to scavange rather than hunt, feeding on large carcasses such as those of carrion, deer or cattle.

SMALLEST BIRD OF PREY

The two smallest varieties of hunting birds are the Black-legged falconet and the Bornean falconet. They usually measure between 5-5.6 in (12.7-14.2 cm), including a 2 in (5 cm) tail, and weigh about 1.25 oz (35 g). The Black-legged falconet is found primarily in southeast Asia, while the Bornean falconet is found in north-western Borneo. They have pointed wings and rounded tails. They also have heavy beaks with teeth inside their mouths. They have sharp talons which help them to hunt.

Did you know?

The highest flying bird is the Ruppell's Griffon vulture. It has been recorded flying at a speed of 22 mph (35 km/h) and a height of 37,000 ft (11,000 m). That is higher than Mount Everest! With a wingspan of 8 ft (2.4 m) these gray brown birds weigh about 15 lbs (6.8 kgs).

BIRD WITH BEST NIGHT VISION AND BEST HEARING

Owls have large eyes and the most powerful night vision of all birds. Like humans, their eyes are in the front of their head, so owls can focus with both their eyes. They can also turn their head 135 degrees in either direction and even look behind their shoulders! But owls are far sighted so they cannot see objects that are close. These nocturnal hunters have an acute sense of hearing. This helps them track the movement of their prey and hunt even in complete darkness. Barn owls and Great Horned owls have the best hearing.

FLIGHTLESS BIRDS

SMALLEST FLIGHTLESS BIRDS

Kiwis are the smallest flightless birds in the world. They have long beaks and no tails. They are indigenous to New Zeland and are the national symbol. The smallest species of kiwi is the Little Spotted kiwi, at no more than 9.8 in (25 cm) tall and weighing 2.8 lbs (1.3 kg). The largest are the Great Spotted kiwis, with a height of 18 in (45 cm) and weight of 7.2 lbs (3.3 kg). Owing to their small size Little Spotted kiwis have been prone to predators and today they are an endangered species!

SMALLEST PENGUIN

The smallest penguin is the African penguin. They are usually found in the coastal regions of southern Africa. These penguins are also known as Jackass penguins because of the donkey-like sound they make! They are about 2 ft (60 cm) tall and weigh between 6.8-8 lbs (3.1-3.6 kg). Like Emperor penguins, they have dark backs with lighter bellies. They are distinguished by a pink gland above their eye. Like all penguins, they are good swimmers and feed on fish and squid.

LARGEST PENGUIN

Measuring up to 4 ft (1.2 m) and weighing about 65 lbs (30 kg), Emperor penguins are the largest member of the penguin family. Found in Antarctica, these birds are easily recognized by their black hoods, blue-gray necks, orange ear-patches and bills and yellow breasts. Emperor penguins are also the only birds in the world to breed in the freezing Antarctic winter.

BIGGEST EGG

The ostrich is quite a record making bird! The ostrich lays the biggest eggs of all birds. Each egg is about 6-8 in (15-20 cm) long and weighs about 3 lbs (1.3 kg)! The eggs are laid in communal nests, which are pits dug in the ground.

Did you know?

The common rhea is known to lay as many as 30 eggs at a time! The eggs are yellow or cream in color. Rheas are also known as nandus. The rhea chicks are usually raised by the male bird. Like ostriches, rheas are capable of running very fast. They are mostly found in South American forests.

LARGEST AND FASTEST FLIGHTLESS BIRD

The largest and fastest flightless bird is the ostrich. Ostriches can be as tall as 9 ft (2.7 m). Ostriches are also the heaviest birds, weighing up to 345 lbs (156 kg). They make up for their inability to fly by running very fast and are capable of speeds up to 43 mph (70 km/h). They can live up to 40 years of age in captivity.

SMALLEST CROCODILES

The smallest crocodiles are called Dwarf crocodiles. These crocodiles are usually about 5 ft (1.5 m) in length. They have black bodies with yellow and black spotted bellies. They have armor-like plates on their backs in order to protect them from predators. They also have scales on their bellies to keep them safe. They have long wide snouts. Dwarf crocodiles are usually found in Africa.

LARGEST CROCODILES

Saltwater crocodiles are the world's largest crocodiles with the length of their body ranging between 15.7-18 ft (4.8-5.5 m). Some have even been reported at lengths of 22 ft (7 m)! Saltwater crocodiles weigh about 1,700 lbs (770 kg). These dangerous and aggressive creatures are found in parts of Australia, Southeast Asia and New Guinea.

FASTEST CROCODILES

With the ability to gallop as they run faster, Johnston's crocodiles are the fastest crocodiles in the world. They are also called Australian freshwater crocodiles. These crocodiles can run as fast as 10 mph (16 km/h). They have thin bodies and long narrow snouts which help them to hunt better. Johnston's crocodiles are found in freshwater.

BIGGEST LIZARD

Komodo Dragons are the world's largest lizards, measuring 7.5 ft (2.25 m) long and weighing around 130 lbs (59 kg). They have a very long tail and a fork-like tongue. Their color ranges from gray to red and even green. With poor eyesight and sense of smell, they use their tongues to taste and smell. Komodo Dragons have a potentially deadly bite, not because of their venom, but because of the poisonous bacteria they have in their mouth. They are found on the Komodo islands of Indonesia.

Did you know?

The Spiny-tailed iguana is the fastest moving reptile in the world. They are known to reach speeds of 21 mph (34 km/h). They can be anywhere from 5 to 39 inches (12–99 cm) long. They are usually brown to gray to black in color, with white or off-white bellies. They have scales on their tails.

LARGEST TURTLES

The largest turtles are the Leatherback turtles. These huge turtles are generally 6.5 ft (2 m) long and weigh around 1,322 lbs (600 kg). Usually black in color, they have a leathery skin covering their shell. Their favorite food is jellyfish as well as other soft creatures of the sea. Leatherback turtles are listed under the endangered animals group.

SMALLEST VENOMOUS SNAKE

Namaqua Dwarf adders grow to 8-9 in (20-25 cm) in length and are thought to be the world's smallest venomous snake. They have a small, heart-shaped head with minute eyes. Their backs are usually gray to gray-brown in color, with lighter bellies. They have brown or black spots all over their body. Namaquas are usually found in Namibia in Africa.

SHORTEST SNAKE

Thread snakes are so tiny they resemble a piece of thread. These snakes are quite difficult to find as they occur only in three regions of the world – Barbados, St. Lucia and Martinique. Thread snakes usually have shiny bodies with colors ranging from pink to brown to black. The longest among them measures just 5 in (11 cm). These tiny snakes are also known as Blind snakes because they have very small eyes and poor vision.

LONGEST SNAKE

The reticulated python grows to a length of 17 ft (5 m). Some are also known to grow as long as 27 ft (8.2 m)! The longest python ever recorded was 32 ft (10 m) long! These huge snakes have backward curving teeth, with which they can hold on to their prey. But they do not kill their prey by biting them. Rather, they wrap their long and strong body around the prey and crush them. Reticulated pythons have diamond-shaped marks on their body, of many different colors and sizes. These nocturnal snakes are predominantly found in Southeast Asia.

LONGEST FANGS

The fangs of the Gaboon viper grow to a length of 2 in (5 cm). Usually folded inside their mouths to keep them from piercing themselves, the fangs unfold only when the snake strikes its prey. They do not have very poisonous venom but are able to release large quantities of it into their prey with the help of their fangs. These vipers can grow up to 7 ft (2 m) long and weigh about 18 lbs (8 kg). They have very large, triangular-shaped heads and a very narrow neck. They have two horns above their nostrils. Their bodies are white or cream in color with black, brown and yellow markings. Their coloration helps them blend in with their surroundings. They are usually found in parts of Africa.

Did you know?

The largest venomous snakes in the world are King cobras. They can grow to 18.5 ft (5.7 m) in length. They have hollow fangs which are 0.5 in (1.25 cm) long. When these deadly snakes are threatened they flatten their necks to form menacing hoods and hiss loudly to scare away their enemies.

FASTEST SNAKE

The fastest snake in the world is the Black mamba. They can reach top speeds of about 12 mph (19 km/h). They are usually gray in color. They get their name from the color of the insides of their mouth, which is black. Black mambas are the second largest poisonous snakes and can grow to 14 ft (4.3 m). Indeed, the venom from one bite would be enough to kill 20 men. They are able to raise about a third of their body into the air, which they do to warn predators away. Black mambas are mainly found in the tropical regions of Africa.

HEAVIEST SNAKE

The heaviest snakes in the world are the anacondas of the South American rainforest. These snakes are generally 20 ft (6 m) long and weigh about 235 lbs (107 kg). There have been unconfirmed reports of anacondas as long as 30 ft (9 m). Anacondas have elastic jaws to help them stretch their mouths really wide. This allows them to swallow prey bigger than themselves in size. They have been known to consume animals as big as deer. These snakes also have curved teeth that grow backward to help them hold on to their prey, but they are not poisonous and use constriction to kill their prey. They wrap themselves around their prey and crush them to death.

SHORTEST LIFESPAN

Newts typically have a lifespan of only 6 years, which is quite low as compared to other amphibians. Newts are tiny salamanders that thrive in marshes, woodland, parks and gardens. Many newts produce toxins in their skin secretions as a defense against predators. The Rough -skinned newt of the Pacific Northwest produces enough tetrodotoxin to kill an adult human.

LARGEST AMPHIBIAN

The Chinese Giant salamander grows to 3.9 ft (1.14 m) in length and weighs between 55 lbs (25-30 kg). They have long tails and very short legs. Their skin is wrinkly in appearance but smooth to touch. They have small eyes and their nostrils are located on their large heads. These huge salamanders do not like to hunt for their food. So they just wait for an animal to come close enough to catch it easily. They are fond of living in cold water streams and are indigenous to China.

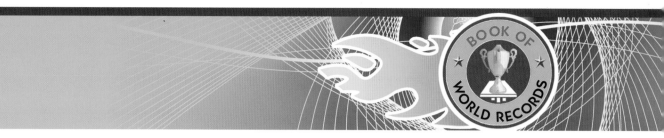

FASTEST FROG

The fastest frog is thought to be the Green frog. They are usually 2-4 in (5-10 cm) in length. Despite their name, these frogs are not always green in color and are often brown and bronze, or even blue! These nocturnal creatures are usually found in warm and humid regions. They prefer living in swamps with plenty of vegetation around. They spend most of their time in water.

SMALLEST AMPHIBIAN

The world's smallest amphibian is the Yellow-striped Pygmy Eleuth frog. Adult males have been recorded as small as 0.3 in (8.4 cm) in length. Their color varies from orange to dark brown with black and yellow markings on their back. These tiny frogs are found in Cuba.

LARGEST FROG

Measuring 13 in (33 cm) long, the African Goliath frog is the largest frog in the world. It can weigh as much as 8 lbs (3.6 kg)! African Goliath frogs can leap as high as 10 ft (3 m) and as far as 20 ft (6 m)! They have a very long fourth toe and will play dead when they feel they are in danger. They are fond of living in fast flowing streams with sandy bottoms. They are found only in regions of West Africa.

Did you know?

Poison Arrow frogs have extremely toxic skin and their bright colors warn predators not to eat them! Poison Arrow frogs are found mostly in the Amazonian rainforests. They are also called Poison Dart frogs because some South American Tribes traditionally used the frog's poison to tip their darts.

INSECTS AND ARACHNIDS

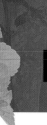

HEAVIEST SPIDER

The female Birdeating spider is possibly the heaviest spider in the world. The heaviest recorded had a body weight of 4.3 oz (122.2 g). These spiders can measure 12 in (30 cm) from leg-tip to leg-tip and have fangs up to 1 in (2.5 cm) in length. Although these spiders carry venom in their fangs, they are not very harmful to humans. Their bite usually causes no more pain than a bee sting. These huge spiders only bite humans when provoked. Their diet includes young birds as well as lizards, frogs, beetles, bats and small snakes.

FASTEST MOVING INSECT

American cockroaches are known to run small distances with incredible speeds of up to 3.4 mph (1.5 metres per second). This is commonly thought to be the record, although there are reports of an Australian tiger beetle capable of 5.57 mph (2.49 m/s)! American cockroaches are extremely hardy. They can survive without any food for months. They also have the ability to slow down their heart beat. They have even been shown to be highly resistant to radiation!

FASTEST FLYING BUTTERFLY

Monarch butterflies are the fastest flying butterflies. They can fly at speeds of up to 17 mph (27.4 km/h). They have beautiful wings that are orange and black, with white spots on the edges. These large butterflies have a wingspan of about 3.4-4.9 in (8.6-12.4 cm). These pretty butterflies are actually poisonous and if consumed they can cause serious illness. They become toxic by eating the leaves of the poisonous milkweed. Some of them migrate over a long distance and it may take them up to three generations to return to their original home. Others spend their whole lives in one place.

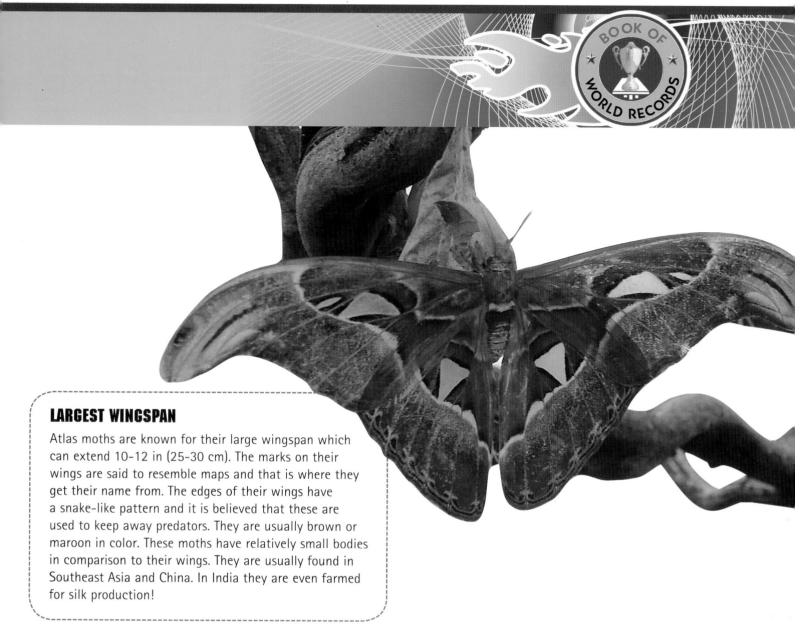

LARGEST WINGSPAN

Atlas moths are known for their large wingspan which can extend 10-12 in (25-30 cm). The marks on their wings are said to resemble maps and that is where they get their name from. The edges of their wings have a snake-like pattern and it is believed that these are used to keep away predators. They are usually brown or maroon in color. These moths have relatively small bodies in comparison to their wings. They are usually found in Southeast Asia and China. In India they are even farmed for silk production!

Did you know?

The mayfly has the shortest lifespan among all insects. They are known to live for as little as 30 minutes to 1 day! These insects are usually found around waterbodies. Due to their short lifespans they are also known as dayflies.

LOUDEST INSECT

African cicadas make a high pitched noise which can reach 106.7 decibles over a distance of about 1.6 ft (0.5 m). This chirping sound is made by the males by rubbing together two membranes, which look like drums. The sound is a mating call to attract female African cicadas. These insects also have a very long lifespan. They are known to live as long as 17 years, which is exceptionally long for an insect. They are found in tropical and temperate regions.

DINOSAUR WITH THE BEST ARMOUR

The Ankylosaurus is thought to have been the most armor-protected dinosaur. They had hard leathery skin with thick plates. They also had two rows of sharp spikes on their back, a tail with a massive club and horn at the back of the head. Two bony plates even protected their eyes. These well-protected dinosaurs were only vulnerable on their underbellies, where they did not have plates. The Ankylosaurus could protect itself from even the ferocious Tyrannosaurus rex.

Did you know?

Antarctosauruses are thought to have been the heaviest dinosaurs, weighing about 100,000 lbs (45,000 kg). A complete skeleton of this species has not been found yet, so it is not possible to know their exact size. But they were probably longer than 60 ft (18 m).

LARGEST MEAT-EATING DINOSAUR

The Giganotosaurus was the largest meat-eating dinosaur and lived between 100 million and 95 million years ago. These huge creatures were 44-46 ft (13.5-14.3 m) long and weighed around 8 tons (7.26 tonnes). They had 8 in (20 cm) long teeth and their skulls were about 6 ft (1.8 m) in length! These enormous meat-eaters preyed on the huge plant-eating dinosaurs and are believed to have been even larger than the Tyrannosaurus rex. But they are thought to have had smaller, banana-shaped brains.

THICKEST SKULL

The Pachycephalosaurus had a head that looked like a dome. The head was made up of bones and was about 8 in (20 cm) thick. These plant-eating dinosaurs had small brains and large eyes. They lived about 76 million to 65 million years ago. The domes on their heads were previously thought to have been used for head-butting, but this is now disputed. Rather, it is more probable that the dome was used for attacking other dinosaurs from the side.

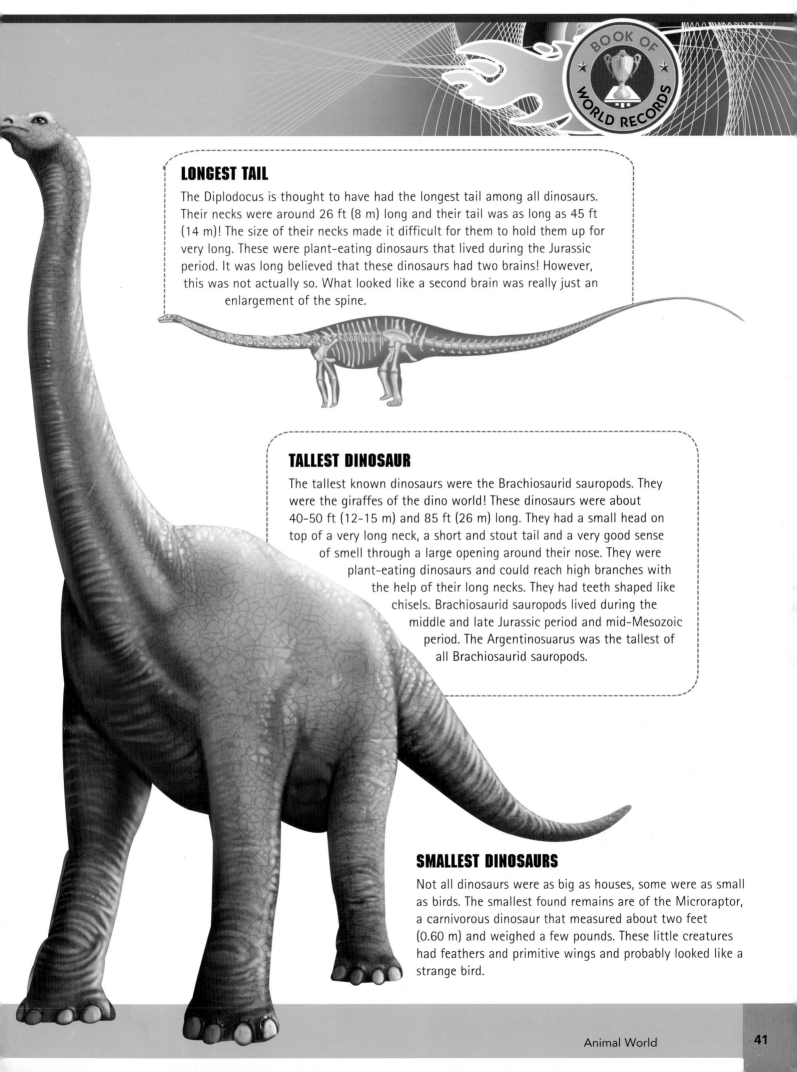

LONGEST TAIL

The Diplodocus is thought to have had the longest tail among all dinosaurs. Their necks were around 26 ft (8 m) long and their tail was as long as 45 ft (14 m)! The size of their necks made it difficult for them to hold them up for very long. These were plant-eating dinosaurs that lived during the Jurassic period. It was long believed that these dinosaurs had two brains! However, this was not actually so. What looked like a second brain was really just an enlargement of the spine.

TALLEST DINOSAUR

The tallest known dinosaurs were the Brachiosaurid sauropods. They were the giraffes of the dino world! These dinosaurs were about 40-50 ft (12-15 m) and 85 ft (26 m) long. They had a small head on top of a very long neck, a short and stout tail and a very good sense of smell through a large opening around their nose. They were plant-eating dinosaurs and could reach high branches with the help of their long necks. They had teeth shaped like chisels. Brachiosaurid sauropods lived during the middle and late Jurassic period and mid-Mesozoic period. The Argentinosuarus was the tallest of all Brachiosaurid sauropods.

SMALLEST DINOSAURS

Not all dinosaurs were as big as houses, some were as small as birds. The smallest found remains are of the Microraptor, a carnivorous dinosaur that measured about two feet (0.60 m) and weighed a few pounds. These little creatures had feathers and primitive wings and probably looked like a strange bird.

PREHISTORIC ANIMALS

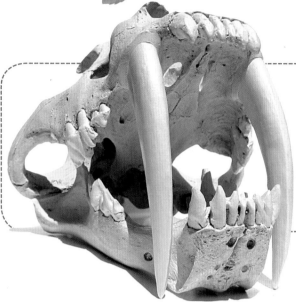

DEADLIEST TEETH OF THE ICE AGE

The deadliest teeth of the Ice Age belonged to a group of animals called Sabre-toothed cats. They had very powerful jaws with extremely sharp teeth. Of particular note were the two huge canine teeth these cats had. They could be as long as 7 in (18 cm)! Sabre-toothed cats were strong and aggressive predators and they are thought to have hunted animals as big as mammoths.

LARGEST PREHISTORIC SHARK

The Megalodon was the largest carnivore of the oceans from 16 million to 1.6 million years ago. They had massive, powerful jaws that were more than 6.5 ft (2 m) wide. They could grow up to 52 ft (16 m) in length, and had sharp teeth, which were about 8.3 in (21 cm) long. In fact, the terrifying great white shark itself is only half the size of the Megalodon. The Megalodon's fin alone was as tall as a full-grown human!

Did you know?

The Indricotherium is the largest prehistoric land animal known. They were the ancestors of the modern-day rhinoceros, but they did not have horns. The Indricotherium was about 20-23 ft (6-7 m) long. The smallest land animal in prehistoric times was a marsupial called Nusculodelphis.

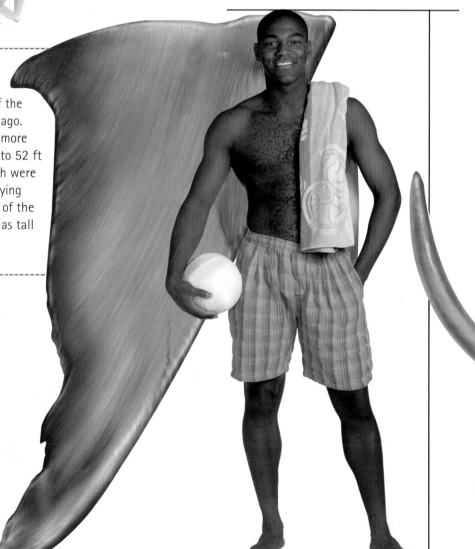

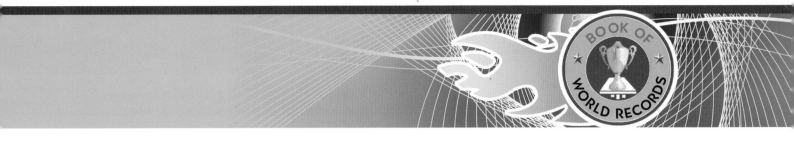

BIGGEST PREHISTORIC LION

The biggest prehistoric lion was the Cave lion. These were much larger than the lions of today, growing to around 11.5 ft (3.5 m) in length. Many drawings of this lion have been found in caves. They were mostly found in Europe and existed until around 20 centuries ago.

LARGEST SLOTH

The huge Megatherium was around 20 ft (6 m) long and weighed about 3-4 tons (2.7-3.6 tonnes). They were plant-eating mammals that walked on four limbs. They had sharp claws on each limb that looked like hooks. Megatheriums were stout creatures with a thick tail and moved very slowly. They existed around 11,000 years ago in South America.

LARGEST MAMMOTH

Mammoths were prehistoric relatives of modern day elephants. They had a huge pair of tusks, which were either straight or curved. The largest Mammoth was the Imperial Mammoth, whose tusks could be as long as 13 ft (4 m). Mammoths used their tusks to fight off enemies as well as to dig out food from under the snow. Some mammoths had lots of hair and fur on their bodies to keep them warm. They were plant-eating animals that lived from 2 million to 9,000 years ago.

Aggressive: Threatening behavior

Agile: Quick and swift

Carnivore: Animals that feed on other animals

Cartilaginous: Fish, like sharks, that have skeletons made not of bone but soft, rubbery tissue or cartilage

Dwindled: Lessened

Endangered: Animals that are in danger of dying out

Ferocious: Scary; frightening

Herbivore: Animal that feeds on plants

Knuckle walking: To move around on all four limbs putting the weight of the whole body on the knuckles

Mammals: Warm blooded animals in which the females produce milk to feed the young

Marsupials: The group of mammals where the mother carries their young is a special pouch after birth

Migrate: To move in large groups from one place to another in search of better weather and food

Mild temperament: Friendly

Nocturnal: Animals that are active at night

Omnivore: Animal that feeds on meat and plants

Pinniped: Mammals that have flippers instead of limbs that they use to swim as well as move on land

Plankton: Small and microscopic organisms drifting or floating in water

Predators: Animals that hunt other animals for food

Reptiles: Cold blooded animals that lay eggs

Retractable: Capable of being drawn or pulled back

Rodents: Small mammals that have a pair of two continuously growing incisors

Stab: To pierce with something pointed

Tetrodotoxin (TTX): A potent toxin, with no known antidote

Vertebrae: Bones that make up the backbone (spinal column)